THE USBORNE
FIRST
THOUSAND
WORDS
IN RUSSIAN

Heather Amery
Illustrated by Stephen Cartwright

Revised edition by Mairi Mackinnon
Picture editing by Mike Olley
Russian language consultant: Katerina Burgess
with thanks to Jonathan Melmoth

D1160405

There is a little yellow duck to look for on every
double page with pictures. Can you find it?

Stephen Cartwright's little yellow duck made his first-ever appearance in *The First Thousand Words* over thirty years ago. Duck has since featured in over 125 titles, in more than 70 languages, and has delighted millions of readers, both young and old, around the world.

This revised edition first published in 2013 by Usborne Publishing Ltd, 83-85 Saffron Hill, London EC1N 8RT. www.usborne.com
Based on a previous title first published in 1979. Copyright © 2013, 1995, 1979 Usborne Publishing Ltd.

About this book

The First Thousand Words in Russian is an enormously popular book that has helped many thousands of children and adults learn new words and improve their Russian language skills.

You'll find it easy to learn words by looking at the **small labelled pictures**. Then you can practise the words by talking about the large central pictures. There is a guide under each word in Russian, showing you how to pronounce it. You can also **hear the words** on the Usborne Quicklinks website: just go to **www.usborne.com/quicklinks** and enter the keywords **1000 russian**. There you can find links to other useful websites about Russia and the Russian language.

There is an alphabetical **word list** at the back of the book, which you can use to look up words in the picture pages.

Remember, this is a book of a thousand words. It will take time to learn them all.

The Russian alphabet

Russian is written in the Cyrillic (say *sirilick*) alphabet. This may look strange at first, but it is fairly easy to learn, and you will soon find that a good many Russian words are actually quite similar to English. For example, a mask is маска, "maska", and a lamp is лампа, "lampa". Once you are familiar with the alphabet, you will be surprised by the number of words you recognize.

Vowels

printed	written			
А а	А *а*	*a* as in *mat*
О о	О *о*	*aw* as in *paw*
Э э	Э *э*	*e* as in *bed*
У у	У *у*	*oo* as in *boot*
Ы ы	Ы *ы*	*i* as in *rip* (tongue pushed back)

printed	written			
Я я	Я *я*	*ya* as in *yak*
Ё ё	Ё *ё*	*yaw* as in *yawn*
Е е	Е *е*	*ye* as in *yet*
Ю ю	Ю *ю*	*yoo* as in *useful*
И и	И *и*	*ee* as in *meet*
Й й	Й *й*	*y* as in *boy*

Consonants

printed	written			
Б б	Б *б*	*b* as in *book*
В в	В *в*	*v* as in *van*
Г г	Г *г*	*g* as in *get*
Д д	D *g*	*d* as in *day*
Ж ж	Ж *ж*	*zh* like the *s* in *pleasure*
З з	З *з*	*z* as in *zoo*
К к	К *к*	*k* as in *kit*
Л л	Л *л*	*l* as in *table*, before a hard vowel, or as in *leaf*, before a soft vowel
М м	М *м*	*m* as in *milk*
Н н	Н *н*	*n* as in *net*

printed	written			
П п	П *п*	*p* as in *pot*
Р р	Р *р*	*r* as in *rock*
С с	С *с*	*s* as in *sit*
Т т	Т *т̄*	*t* as in *top*
Ф ф	Ф *ф*	*f* as in *fan*
Х х	Х *х*	*ch* as in Scottish *loch*
Ц ц	Ц *ц*	*ts* as in *cats*
Ч ч	Ч *ч*	*ch* as in *cheese*
Ш ш	Ш *ш*	*sh* as in *fresh*
Щ щ	Щ *щ*	*shch* as in *fresh cheese*
Ъ ъ	Ъ *ъ*	'hard sign' (very rare), gives the letter before it a 'hard' sound.
Ь ь	Ь *ь*	'soft sign', gives the letter before it a 'soft' sound.

You'll find more **tips on reading and pronouncing Russian words** at the beginning of the word list, at the back of the book.

краски
kraskee

бутылки
boo**til**kee

золотые рыбки
zolo**tiy**e **rib**kee

вертолёт
vyerta**lyot**

картинка-конструктор
kar**teen**ka-kan**strook**tar

шоколад
shaka**lat**

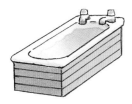

ванна
vanna

мыло
mila

кран
kran

туалетная бумага
tooa**lyet**-naya boo**ma**ga

зубная щётка
zoo**bna**ya **shchot**ka

вода
va**da**

унитаз
oonee**tas**

губка
goopka

раковина
rakaveena

душ
doosh

полотенце
pala**tyen**tse

Дома **do**ma

кровать
kra**vat'**

ванная
vannaya

ГОСТИНАЯ
ga**stee**naya

4

зубная паста
zoo**bna**ya **pas**ta

радио
radeeo

подушка
pa**doosh**ka

DVD-диск
dee-vee-dee
deesk

ковёр
ka**vyor**

софа
sa**fa**

СТУЛ
stool

пуховое одеяло
poo**ho**vaye adye**ya**la

расчёска
ras**chos**ka

простыня
prasti**nya**

коврик
kovreek

ШКАФ
shkaf

телевизор
tele**veez**ar

КОМОД
ka**mot**

СПАЛЬНЯ
аl'nya

зеркало
zyerkala

щётка
shchotka

ЛАМПА
lampa

ОЛЛ
oll

картины
kar**tee**ni

вешалка
vyeshalka

телефон
tele**fon**

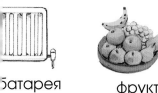

Батарея
bata**rye**ya

фрукты
frookty

газета
ga**zye**ta

СТОЛ
stol

письма
pees'ma

лестница
lyesneetsa

5

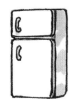

ХОЛОДИЛЬНИК
hala**deel'**neek

СТАКАНЫ
sta**ka**ni

ЧАСЫ
cha**si**

ТАБУРЕТ
taboo**ryet**

ЧАЙНЫЕ ЛОЖКИ
chayniye **lozh**kee

ВЫКЛЮЧАТЕЛЬ
viklyoo-**cha**tyel'

СТИРАЛЬНЫЙ ПОРОШОК
stee**ral'**niy para**shok**

КЛЮЧ
klyooch

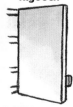

ДВЕРЬ
dver'

Кухня  **kooh**nya

МОЙКА
moyka

ПЫЛЕСОС
pilye**sos**

КАСТРЮЛИ
ka**stryoo**lee

ВИЛКИ
veelkee

ФАРТУК
fartook

ГЛАДИЛЬНАЯ ДОСКА
gla**deel'**naya das**ka**

МУСОР
moosar

ЧАЙНИК
chayneek

НОЖИ
nazhee

ШВАБРА
shvabra

ТРЯПКА ДЛЯ ПЫЛИ
tryapka dlya pilee

КАФЕЛЬ
kafyel'

ЩЁТКА
shchotka

СТИРАЛЬНАЯ МАШИНА
steeral'naya masheena

СОВОК
savok

ЯЩИК
yashcheek

БЛЮДЦА
blyootsa

СКОВОРОДА
skavarada

ПЛИТА
pleeta

ЛОЖКИ
loshkee

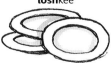

ТАРЕЛКИ
taryelkee

УТЮГ
ootyook

КЛАДОВКА
kladofka

УХОННОЕ ПОЛОТЕНЦЕ
oohannaye palatyentse

ЧАШКИ
chashkee

СПИЧКИ
speechkee

ЩЁТКА
shchotka

МИСКИ
meeskee

7

Сад sat

тачка
tachka

улей
ooley

улитка
oo**leet**ka

кирпичи
keerpee**chee**

голубь
goloop'

лопата
la**pa**ta

божья коровка
bozh'ya ka**rof**ka

мусорный бак
moosarniy **bak**

семена
syeme**na**

сарай
sa**ray**

лейка
leyka

червяк
cher**vyak**

цветы
tsvye**ti**

поливальная
установка
palee-**val'**naya oosta**nof**ka

мотыга
ma**tig**a

оса
a**sa**

8

пчела
pchye**la**

СОВОК
sa**vok**

КОСТЬ
kost'

ЖИВАЯ ИЗГОРОДЬ
zhi**va**ya **eez**garat'

ВИЛЫ
veeli

ГАЗОНОКОСИЛКА
gazona-ka**seel**ka

ТРОПИНКА
tra**peen**ka

ЛИСТЬЯ
leest'ya

ДЕРЕВО
deryeva

ДЫМ
dim

ГУСЕНИЦА
goosyeneetsa

ГРАБЛИ
grablee

ГНЕЗДО
gnyez**do**

ВЕТКИ
vyetkee

ТЕПЛИЦА
tye**pleet**sa

ТРАВА
tra**va**

КОЛЯСКА
ka**lyas**ka

ОВОЩИ
ovashchi

КОСТЁР
ka**styor**

ШЛАНГ
shlank

9

Мастерская

шурупы
shooroopi

ТИСКИ
teeskee

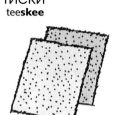
наждачная бумага
nazhdachnaya boomaga

дрель
dryel'

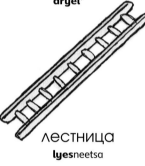
лестница
lyesneetsa

пила
peela

ОПИЛКИ
apeelkee

календарь
kalyendar'

ящик для инструментов
yashcheek dlya eenstroomyentaf

отвёртка
atvyortka

доска
daska

стружки
strooshkee

перочинный нож
pyeracheenniy nosh

10

КНОПКИ
knopkee

ПАУК
pa-**ook**

ВИНТЫ
vee**nti**

ГАЙКИ
gaykee

ПАУТИНА
pa-oo**tee**na

бочка
bochka

муха
mooha

топор
ta**por**

рулетка
roo**lyet**ka

МОЛОТОК
mala**tok**

НАПИЛЬНИК
na**peel'**neek

банка с
краской
banka s**kras**koy

рубанок
roo**ba**nak

дрова
dra**va**

ГВОЗДИ
gvozdee

ВЕРСТАК
vyer**stak**

банки
bankee

11

Улица

ooleetsa

магазин
maga**zeen**

яма
yama

кафе
ka-**fe**

скорая помощь
skoraya **po**mashch'

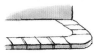

тротуар
trato**oar**

памятник
pam**yat**neek

труба
troo**ba**

крыша
krisha

экскаватор
ekska**va**tar

12 гостиница
gas**tee**neetsa

автобус
af**to**boos

мужчина
moozh**chee**na

полицейская
машина
pali**tsey**skaya ma**shee**na

трубы
troobi

отбойный
молоток
at**boy**niy mala**tok**

школа
shkola

площадка
для игр
plash**chat**ka dlya eeg

такси
tak**see**

переход
pere**hot**

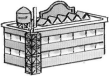
фабрика
fabreeka

грузовик
grooza**veek**

светофор
svyeta**for**

кинотеатр
keenate**atr**

фургон
foor**gon**

каток
ka**tok**

прицеп
pree**tsep**

дом
dom

рынок
rinak

лестница
lestneetsa

мотоцикл
mata**tseek**l

...осипед
...lasee**pyet**

пожарная машина
pa**zhar**naya ma**shee**na

полицейский
pali**tsey**skeey

машина
ma**shee**na

женщина
zhenshcheena

уличный фонарь
ooleechniy fa**nar'**

здание
zdaneeye

13

железная дорога
zhe**lyez**naya
da**ro**ga

игральные кости
ee**gral'**niye
kostee

блок-флейта
blok-**fley**ta

робот
robat

ожерелье
azhe**ryel'**ye

фотоаппарат
fota-appa**rat**

бусы
boosi

куклы
kookli

гитара
gee**ta**ra

кольцо
kal'**tso**

КУКОЛЬНЫЙ ДОМ
kookal'niy **dom**

Магазин игрушек

maga**zeen**
ee**groo**shek

губная гармошка
goo**bna**ya gar**mosh**ka

СВИСТОК
svee**stok**

КУБИКИ
koobeekee

ЗАМОК
zamak

ПОДВОДНАЯ ЛОДКА
pad**vod**naya **lod**ka

труба
troo**ba**

стрел
stryeli

14

лук
look

парашют
para**shoot**

яхта
yahta

грим
greem

каток
ka**tok**

маски
maskee

гоночная машина
gonachnaya ma**shee**na

лошадь-качалка
loshad'-ka**chal**ka

копилка
ka**peel**ka

шарики
shareekee

марионетки
mareea-**nyet**kee

рояль
ra**yal'**

космонавты
kasma**naf**ti

подъёмный
кран
pa**dyom**niy **kran**

игральные
карты
eeg**ral'**niye **kar**ti

барабаны
bara**ba**ni

солдатики
sal**da**teekee

краски
kraskee

ракета
ra**kyet**a

15

качели
ka**chyel**ee

песочница
pe**soch**neetsa

ПИКНИК
peek**neek**

воздушный
змей
vaz**doosh**niy
z**myey**

мороженое
ma**ro**zhenaye

собака
sa**ba**ka

КАЛИТКА
ka**leet**ka

тропинка
tra**peen**ka

лягушка
lya**goosh**ka

Парк **park**

скамейка
ska**myey**ka

16 горка для катания
gorka dlya ka**ta**neeya

головастики
gala**vas**teekee

озеро
ozyera

РОЛИКИ
roleekee

КУСТ
koost

МАЛЫШ
ma**lish**

СКЕЙТБОРД
skeytbort

ЗЕМЛЯ
zyem**lya**

ПРОГУЛОЧНАЯ КОЛЯСКА
pra**goo**-lachnaya ka**lyas**ka

КАЧЕЛИ
ka**chyel**ee

ДЕТИ
dyetee

ТРЁХКОЛЁСНЫЙ ВЕЛОСИПЕД
tryohkal-**yos**niy vyela-see**pyet**

ПТИЦЫ
pteetsi

ЗАБОР
za**bor**

МЯЧ
myach

ЯХТА
yahta

БЕЧЁВКА
bye**chof**ka

ЛУЖА
loozha

УТЯТА
ootya**ta**

СКАКАЛКА
ska**kal**ka

ДЕРЕВЬЯ
dye**ryev'**ya

КЛУМБА
kloomba

ЛЕБЕДИ
lyebedee

ПОВОДОК
pava**dok**

УТКИ
ootkee

17

Животные

zhi**vot**niye

панда
panda

крыло
kri**lo**

орёл
ar**yol**

бегемот
bege**mot**

летучая мышь
lye**too**chaya **mish'**

горилла
ga**reel**la

лапы
lapi

обезьяна
abyez**'ya**na

кенгуру
kengoo**roo**

хвост
hvost

ВОЛК
volk

айсберг
aysbyerk

пингвин
peen**gveen**

перья
pyer'ya

крокодил
kraka**deel**

медведь
myed**vyet'**

пеликан
pelee**kan**

страус
straoos

дельфин
dyel'**feen**

лев
lyef

львята
l'**vya**ta

жираф
zhi**raf**

олень
alen'

верблюд
vyerblyoot

тюлень
tyoolen'

белый медведь
byeliy myedvyet'

черепаха
cherepaha

хобот
hobat

носорог
nasarok

бизон
beezon

рожки
rozhkee

слон
slon

бобр
bobr

коза
kaza

зебра
zyebra

змея
zmeya

акула
akoola

кит
keet

тигр
teegr

леопард
lyeapart

19

Путешествие

pootye-**shest**veeye

**железная
дорога**
zhe**lyez**naya
da**ro**ga

ЛОКОМОТИВ
lakama**teef**

буфера
boofye**ra**

ВАГОНЫ
va**go**ni

машинист
mashee**neest**

товарный поезд
ta**var**niy **po**yest

платформа
plat**for**ma

контролёр
kantra**lyor**

чемодан
chema**dan**

**касса-
автомат**
kassa-afta**mat**

20

Вокзал vak**zal**

Гараж ga**rash**

семафор
sema**for**

рюкзак
ryook**zak**

фары
fari

двигатель
dveegatyel'

колесо
kaly**eso**

аккумуля
akoomoo-l**y**

самолёт
samalyot

вертолёт
vyertalyot

взлётная полоса
vslyotnaya palasa

диспетчерская вышка
deespyetcherskaya vishka

стюарды
styooardy

пилот
peelot

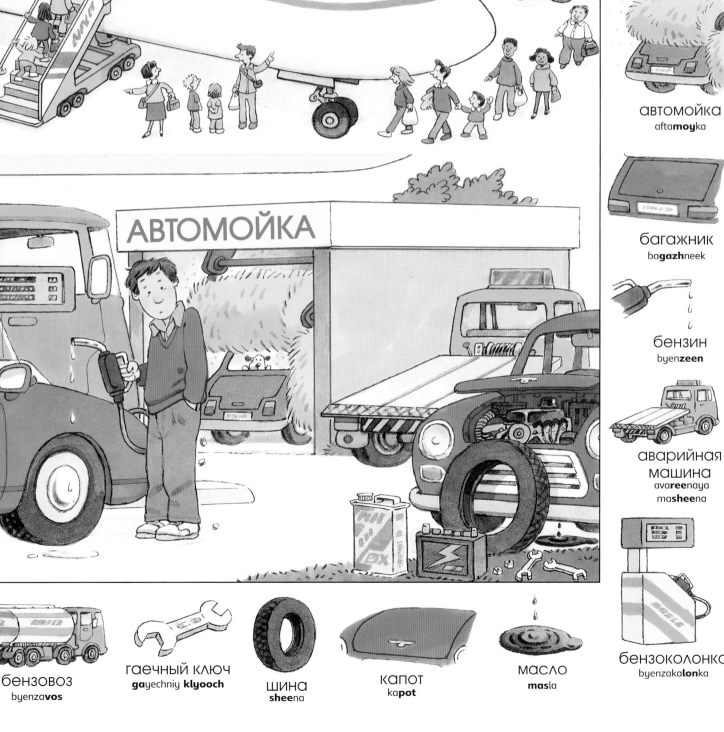

автомойка
aftamoyka

АВТОМОЙКА

багажник
bagazhneek

бензин
byenzeen

аварийная машина
avareenaya masheena

бензовоз
byenzavos

гаечный ключ
gayechniy klyooch

шина
sheena

капот
kapot

масло
masla

бензоколонка
byenzakalonka

21

Сельская местность

ветряная мельница
vyetrya-naya myel'neetsa

воздушный шар
vazdooshniy shar

бабочка
babachka

ящерица
yashchereetsa

камни
kamnee

лиса
leesa

ручей
roochey

дорожный указатель
darozhniy ookazatyel'

ёж
yosh

шлюз
shlyoos

22

гора
gara

белка
byelka

лес
lyes

барсук
barsook

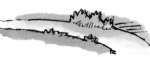

река
ryeka

дорога
daroga

палатки
pa**lat**kee

канал
ka**nal**

брёвна
bryovna

деревня
de**ryev**nya

МОТЫЛЁК
mati**lyok**

МОСТ
most

баржа
barzha

ВОДОПАД
vada**pat**

СОВА
sa**va**

туннель
too**nel'**

ЛИСЯТА
lee**sya**ta

крот
krot

рыбак
ri**bak**

ХОЛМ
holm

КАМНИ
kamnee

жаба
zhaba

поезд
poyest

автофургон
aftafoor**gon**

23

Ферма **fyer**ma

стог
stok

колли
kollee

ягнята
yag**nya**ta

пруд
proot

цыплята
tsi**plya**ta

чердак
cher**dak**

свинарник
svee**nar**neek

бык
bik

курятник
koo**ryat**neek

24 трактор
traktar

петух
pye**tooh**

гуси
goosee

цистерна
tsees**ter**na

амбар
am**bar**

земля
zyem**lya**

тележка
tye**lyesh**ka

фермер
fyermyer

поле
polye

куры
koori

телёнок
tye**lyo**nak

забор
za**bor**

седло
syed**lo**

КОРОВНИК
ka**rov**neek

корова
ka**rov**a

ПЛУГ
plook

САД
sat

КОНЮШНЯ
ka**nyoosh**nya

поросята
para**sya**ta

осёл
as**yol**

ИНДЮКИ
eendyoo**kee**

пугало
poogala

дом на ферме
dom na **fyer**mye

сено
syena

ОВЦЫ
oftsi

брикеты соломы
bree**kyet**i sa**lo**mi

ЛОШАДЬ
loshat'

СВИНЬИ
sveen'ee

25

парусник
paroosneek

море
morye

весло
vyes**lo**

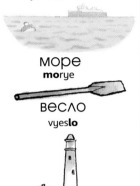

маяк
ma**yak**

лопата
la**pa**ta

ведро
vye**dro**

морская звезда
mar**ska**ya zvyez**da**

замок из песка
zamak eez pyes**ka**

зонтик
zonteek

флаг
flak

моряк
ma**ryak**

У моря oo **mo**rya

ракушка
ra**koo**shka

краб
krap

чайка
chayka

остров
ostraf

катер
katyer

водный лыжн
vodniy **lizh**neek

ВОЛНЫ
volni

ШЛЯПА
shlyapa

УТЁС
oo**tyos**

КОРАБЛЬ
ka**rabl'**

БАЙДАРКА
bay**dar**ka

КАНАТ
ka**nat**

ГАЛЬКА
gal'ka

ВОДОРОСЛИ
vodaraslee

СЕТЬ
syet'

ВЕСЛО
vyes**lo**

РЫБАЧЬЯ ЛОДКА
ri**bach'**ya **lot**ka

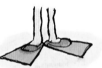
ЛАСТЫ
lasti

ЛОСЬОН
las**yon**

РЫБА
riba

...ПАЛЬНИК
...o**pal'**neek

ТАНКЕР
tankyer

ПЛЯЖ
plyash

ВЁСЕЛЬНАЯ ЛОДКА
vyosel'naya **lot**ka

ШЕЗЛОНГ
shez**lonk**

НОЖНИЦЫ
nozhneetsi

$2 + 2 = 4$
$2 + 3 = 5$

ПРИМЕРЫ
pree**myer**i

РЕЗИНКА
rye**zeen**ka

ЛИНЕЙКА
lee**nyey**ka

ФОТОГРАФИИ
fata**graf**ee

ФЛОМАСТЕРЫ
fla**mas**teri

ГЛИНА
gleena

КРАСКИ
kraskee

МАЛЬЧИК
mal'cheek

КАРАНДАШ
karan**dash**

В ШКОЛЕ f**shkol**ye

ДОСКА
da**ska**

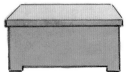

ПИСЬМЕННЫЙ СТОЛ
pees'myenniy stol

КНИГИ
kneegee

РУЧКА
roochka

КЛЕЙ
kley

МЕЛ
myel

РИСУН...
reesoona...

сорное ведро
noosarnaye vye**dro**

учительница
oo**chee**tel'neetsa

коробка
ka**rop**ka

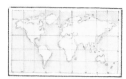
карта
karta

кисточка
keestochka

ПОТОЛОК
pata**lok**

стена
sty**e**na

ПОЛ
pol

тетрадь
tyet**rat'**

абвгдеёжз
ийклмнопр
стуфхцчш
щъыьэюя

алфавит
alfa**veet**

значок
zna**chok**

аквариум
ak**va**reeooom

бумага
boo**ma**ga

жалюзи
zhalyoozee

мольберт
mal'**byert**

абвгдеёжз
ийклмнопр
стуфхцчш
щъыьэюя

ерная ручка
chernaya **rooch**ka

растение
ra**styen**eeye

глобус
globoos

девочка
dyevachka

восковые
мелки
vaska**vi**ye **myel**kee

настольная
лампа
na**stol'**naya **lam**pa

29

Больница bal'**neet**sa

медбрат
myed**brat**

вата
vata

лекарство
lye**kar**stva

лифт
leeft

халат
ha**lat**

костыли
kasti**lee**

таблетки
ta**blyet**kee

поднос
pad**nos**

часы
cha**si**

термометр
tyer**mo**metr

занавеска
zana-**vyes**ka

яблоко
yablako

гипс
geeps

бинт
beent

кресло-каталка
kryesla-ka**tal**ka

картинка-
конструктор
kar**teen**ka-kan**strook**tar

врач
vrach

шприц
shpreets

30

Врач
vrach

шлёпанцы
shlyopantsi

компьютер
kamp'**yoo**ter

пластырь
plastir'

банан
ba**nan**

виноград
veena**grat**

корзина
kar**zee**na

игрушки
ee**groosh**kee

груша
groosha

открытки
at**krit**kee

подгузник
pad**gooz**neek

палка
palka

подушка
pad**oosh**ka

ночная рубашка
nach**na**ya roo**bash**ka

пижама
pee**zha**ma

апельсин
apel'**seen**

салфетки
sal**fyet**kee

комиксы
komeeksi

приёмная
pree**yom**naya

31

воздушный
шарик
vaz**doosh**niy **sha**reek

ШОКОЛАД
shaka**lat**

ОЧКИ
ach**kee**

конфета
kan**fyet**a

ОКНО
ak**no**

фейерверк
feyer**vyerk**

ЛЕНТА
lyenta

ТОРТ
tort

Вечеринка
vyeche**reen**ka

ПОДАРКИ
pa**dar**kee

СОЛОМИНКА
sa**lo**meenka

свеча
svye**cha**

ГИРЛЯНДА
geer**lyan**da

ИГРУШКИ
ee**groosh**kee

32

мандарин
manda**reen**

САЛЯМИ
sa**lya**mee

ПЛЮШЕВЫЙ МИШКА
plyoo**shev**iy **mee**shka

СОСИСКА
sa**sees**ka

ЧИПСЫ
cheepsi

МАСКАРАДНЫЕ КОСТЮМЫ
maska-**rad**niye kas**tyoo**mi

ВИШНЯ
veeshnya

ФРУКТОВЫЙ СОК
frook**to**viy **sok**

МАЛИНА
ma**lee**na

КЛУБНИКА
kloob**nee**ka

ЛАМПОЧКА
lampachka

утерброд
bootyer**brot**

масло
masla

печенье
pye**chen'**ye

СЫР
seer

хлеб
hlyep

скатерть
skatyert'

33

Магазин magazeen

грейпфрут
greypfroot

морковь
markof'

цветная капуста
tsvyetnaya kapoosta

лук-порей
look-parey

гриб
greep

огурец
agooryets

лимон
leemon

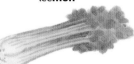

сельдерей
syel'derey

абрикос
abreekos

34 дыня
dinya

пакет
pakyet

сыр

овощи и фрукты

лук
look

капуста
kapoosta

персик
pyerseek

салат
salat

горох
garoh

помидо
pameedo

ЯЙЦА
yaytsa

СЛИВА
sleeva

МУКА
moo**ka**

ВЕСЫ
vye**si**

БАНКИ
bankee

МЯСО
myasa

АНАНАС
ana**nas**

ЙОГУРТ
yogoort

КОРЗИНА
kar**zee**na

БУТЫЛКИ
boo**til**kee

СУМОЧКА
soomachka

КОШЕЛЁК
kashe**lyok**

ДЕНЬГИ
dyen'gee

КОНСЕРВЫ
kan**syer**vi

ТЕЛЕЖКА
tye**lyesh**ka

ртофель
kar**to**fel'

ШПИНАТ
shpee**nat**

БОБЫ
ba**bi**

КАССА
kassa

ТЫКВА
tikva

35

Еда _{yeda}

завтрак
zaftrak

обед
a**byet**

варёное яйцо
va**ryon**aye yay**tso**

кофе
kofye

яичница
ya**eesh**neetsa

тосты
tosti

джем
djem

сливки
sleefkee

молоко
mala**ko**

хлопья
hlop'ya

какао
ka**ka**o

сахар
sahar

мёд
myot

соль
sol'

перец
pyeryets

чай
chay

чайник
chayneek

блины
blee**ni**

булочки
boolachkee

36

ужин
oozheen

ветчина
vyetchee**na**

суп
soop

омлет
am**lyet**

салат
sa**lat**

палочки
palachkee

гамбургер
gamboorgyer

цыплёнок
tsi**plyo**nak

рис
rees

соус
so-oos

спагетти
spa**get**tee

картофельное пюре
kar**to**fel'naye pyoo**re**

пицца
peetsa

чипсы
cheepsi

десерт
de**syert**

Я ya

ГОЛОВА
galava

ВОЛОСЫ
volasi

ЛИЦО
lee**tso**

бровь
brof'

глаз
glas

нос
nos

щека
shche**ka**

рот
rot

губы
goobi

рука
roo**ka**

ЛОКОТЬ
lokat'

ЖИВОТ
zhi**vot**

зубы
zoobi

язык
ya**zik**

подбородок
padba**ro**dak

уши
ooshee

шея
sheya

плечи
plyechee

ПАЛЬЦЫ НОГИ
pal'tsi na**gee**

СТУПНЯ
stoop**nya**

НОГА
na**ga**

КОЛЕНО
ka**lyen**a

грудь
groot'

спина
spee**na**

ягодицы
yaga**deet**si

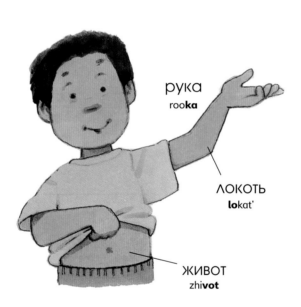

кисть руки
keest' roo**kee**

большой палец
bal'**shoy pa**lyets

пальцы
pal'tsi

Моя одежда maya adyezhda

НОСКИ
naskee

ТРУСЫ
troosee

МАЙКА
mayka

БРЮКИ
bryookee

ДЖИНСЫ
djeensi

ФУТБОЛКА
footbolka

ЮБКА
yoopka

РУБАШКА
roobashka

ГАЛСТУК
galstook

ШОРТЫ
shorti

КОЛГОТКИ
kalgotkee

ПЛАТЬЕ
plat'ye

ДЖЕМПЕР
djempyer

СВИТЕР
sveeter

КОФТА
kofta

ШАРФ
sharf

НОСОВОЙ ПЛАТОК
nasavoy platok

КРОССОВКИ
krassofkee

БОТИНКИ
bateenkee

САНДАЛИИ
sandalee

САПОГИ
sapagee

ПЕРЧАТКИ
pyerchatkee

КАРМАНЫ
karmani

РЕМЕНЬ
ryemen'

ПРЯЖКА
pryashka

МОЛНИЯ
molneeya

ШНУРОК
shnoorok

ПУГОВИЦЫ
poogaveetsi

ПЕТЛИ
pyetlee

ПАЛЬТО
pal'to

КУРТКА
koortka

КЕПКА
kyepka

ШЛЯПА
shlyapa

Люди **lyoo**dee

актёр
ak**tyor**

актриса
ak**tree**sa

повар
povar

танцоры
tan**tsor**i

певцы
pyef**tsi**

космонавт
kazma**naft**

МЯСНИК
myas**neek**

полицейский
pali**tsyey**skiy

женщина-
полицейский
zhenshcheena-
pali**tsyey**skiy

ПЛОТНИК
plotneek

пожарник
pa**zhar**neek

ХУДОЖНИК
hoo**dozh**neek

СУДЬЯ
sood'**ya**

механики
mye**ha**neekee

парикмахер
pareek-**ma**hyer

водитель грузовика
va**dee**tyel' groozavee**ka**

водитель автобуса
va**dee**tyel' av**to**boosa

зубной врач
zoob**noy vrach**

водолаз
vada**las**

почтальон
pachtal'**on**

официант
afee-tsee**ant**

официантка
afee-tsee**ant**ka

маляр
ma**lyar**

пекарь
pyekar'

Семья

syem'**ya**

сын
sin

брат
brat

дочь
doch'

сестра
syes**tra**

мать
mat'

жена
zhe**na**

отец
a**tyets**

муж
moosh

тётя
tyotya

дядя
dyadya

домашнее
животное
da**mash**nyeye
zhi**vot**noye

двоюродный
брат
dva**yoo**radniy **brat**

дедушка
dyedooshka

бабушка
babooshka

Занятия zanyateeya

улыбаться
oolibat'sa

плакать
plakat'

думать
doomat'

слушать
slooshat'

смеяться
smeyat'sa

ловить
laveet'

бросать
brasat'

ломать
lamat'

рисовать
reesavat'

писать
peesat'

рубить
roobeet'

резать
ryezat'

есть
yest'

разговаривать
razga-vareevat'

копать
kapat'

нести
nyestee

пить
peet'

делать
dyelat'

прыгать
prigat'

танцевать
tantsevat'

мыть
mit'

вязать
vyazat'

ползти
palstee

42

играть
eegrat'

смотреть
smatryet'

залезать
zalyezat'

драться
drat'sa

спать
spat'

брать
brat'

прыгать
prigat'

шить
sheet'

ждать
zhdat'

готовить еду
gatoveet' yedoo

прятаться
pryatat'sa

читать
cheetat'

покупать
pakoopat'

толкать
talkat'

петь
pyet'

дуть
doot'

тянуть
tyanoot'

подметать
padmyetat'

собирать
sabeerat'

падать
padat'

идти
eedtee

бежать
byezhat'

сидеть
seedyet'

43

Антонимы
antoneemi

хороший
haroshiy

плохой
plahoy

верхний
vyerhniy

нижний
neezhniy

далеко
dalyeko

близко
bleeska

холодный
halodniy

горячий
garyachiy

мокрый
mokriy

сухой
soohoy

толстый
tolstiy

тонкий
tonkiy

грязный
gryazniy

чистый
cheestiy

над
nat

под
pot

открытый
atkritiy

закрытый
zakritiy

маленький
malyen'kiy

большой
bal'shoy

мало
mala

много
mnoga

первый
pyerviy

последний
paslyedniy

левый
lyeviy

снаружи
snaroozhi

внутри
vnootree

легко
lyehko

трудно
troodna

пустой
poostoy

полный
polniy

мягкий
myahkiy

твёрдый
tvyordiy

спереди
speryedee

высоко
visako

медленно
myedlyenna

быстро
bistra

сзади
szadee

длинный
dleenniy

низко
neezka

короткий
karotkiy

мёртвый
myortviy

живой
zhivoy

темно
tyemno

светло
svyetlo

старый
stariy

наверху
navyerhoo

правый
praviy

новый
noviy

внизу
vneezoo

45

ДНИ dnee

воскресенье
vaskre-**syen'**ye

четверг
chet**vyerk**

вторник
f**tor**neek

суббота
soob**bo**ta

понедельник
panye**dyel'**neek

среда
srye**da**

пятница
pyatneetsa

календарь
kalyen**dar'**

утро
ootra

вечер
vyecher

солнце
sontse

луна
loo**na**

звезда
zvyez**da**

ночь
noch'

космос
kosmas

планета
pla**nyet**a

ракета
ra**kyet**a

телескоп
tyele**skop**

Праздники prazneekee

день рождения
dyen' razh**dyen**eeya

поздравительная
открытка
pazdra-**vee**tel'naya
at**krit**ka

свеча
svye**cha**

отпуск
otpoosk

подарок
pa**da**rak

праздничный торт
prazneechniy **tort**

свадьба
svad'ba

гости
gostee

фотоаппарат
fota-appa**rat**

подружка невесты
pa**droosh**ka nye**vyes**ti

невеста и жених
nye**vyes**ta ee zhe**neeh**

фотограф
fa**to**graf

Рождество
razhdest**vo**

северный
олень
syeverniy
a**len'**

Дед Мороз
dyet ma**ros**

сани
sanee

ёлка
yolka

47

Погода pa**go**da

ЗОНТИК
zonteek

ДОЖДЬ
dosht'

МОЛНИЯ
molneeya

солнце
sontse

облак
oblaka

небо
nyeba

ТУМАН
too**man**

СНЕГ
snyek

роса
ra**sa**

ветер
vyetyer

ТУМАН
too**man**

мороз
ma**ros**

радуга
radooga

Времена года vremye**na go**da

весна
vyes**na**

лето
lyeta

осень
osyen'

зима
zee**ma**

Домашние животные

damashneeye zhivotniye

ветврач
vyetvrach

будка
bootka

хомяк
hamyak

морская свинка
marskaya sveenka

собака
sabaka

щенок
shchenok

волнистый попугай
valneestiy papoo-gay

попугай
papoogay

клюв
klyoof

корм
korm

канарейка
kanaryeyka

кролик
kroleek

клетка
klyetka

кошка
koshka

корзина
karzeena

котёнок
katyonak

молоко
malako

золотые рыбки
zalatiye ripkee

мышь
mish'

49

Спорт и физкультура

парус
paroos

гребля
gryeblya

сноубординг
sno-oo**bor**deenk

баскетбол
baskyet**bol**

парусный спорт
paroosniy **sport**

виндсёрфинг
veend**syor**feenk

крикет
kreekyet

каратэ
kara**te**

бита
beeta

ракетка
ra**kyet**ka

американский
футбол
ameree**kan**skiy
foot**bol**

гимнастика
geem**nas**teeka

мяч
m**yach**

теннис
tennees

удочка
oodachka

наживка
na**zhiv**ka

танцы
tantsi

бейсбол
beys**bol**

рыбалка
ri**bal**ka

регби
regbee

прыжки в воду
prish**kee vvo**doo

бассейн
bas**seyn**

бег
byek

плавание
plavaneeye

50

стрельба
из лука
stryel'**ba**
eez **loo**ka

мишень
mee**shyen'**

дельтапланеризм
dyel'ta-planye**reezm**

бег трусцой
byek troos**tsoy**

шлем
shlyem

велоспорт
vyela**sport**

альпинизм
al'pee**neezm**

дзюдо
dzyoo**do**

лошадь
loshat'

пони
ponee

шкафчик
shkafcheek

футбол
foot**bol**

верховая езда
vyerha**va**ya yez**da**

раздевалка
razdye-**val**ka

коньки
kan'**kee**

бадминтон
badmeen**ton**

настольный тенис
na**stol'niy** **ten**nees

фигурное катание
fee**goor**naye ka**ta**neeye

лыжная
палка
lizhnaya **pal**ka

подъёмник
pa**dyom**neek

борьба сумо
bar'**ba soo**mo

лыжи
lizhee

горка для
катания
gorka **dlya** ka**tan**eeya

51

Цвета tsvyeta

оранжевый
aranjeviy

зелёный
zyelyoniy

чёрный
chorniy

серый
syeriy

красны
krasniy

коричневый
kareechnyeviy

розовый
rozaviy

белый
byeliy

синий
seeniy

пурпурный
poorpoorniy

жёлтый
zholtiy

Фигуры feegoori

прямоугольник
pryama-oogol'neek

круг
krook

ромб
romp

конус
konoos

звезда
zvyezda

куб
koop

овал
aval

треугольник
trye-oogol'neek

квадрат
kvadrat

полумесяц
paloo-myesyats

52

Числа

cheesla

1	один a**deen**	
2	два **dva**	
3	три **tree**	
4	четыре che**tir**ye	
5	пять **pyat'**	
6	шесть **shest'**	
7	семь **syem'**	
8	восемь **vos**yem'	
9	девять **dyev**yat'	
10	десять **dyes**yat'	
11	одиннадцать a**deen**natsat'	
12	двенадцать dvye**nat**sat'	
13	тринадцать tree**nat**sat'	
14	четырнадцать che**tir**-natsat'	
15	пятнадцать pyat**nat**sat'	
16	шестнадцать shest**nat**sat'	
17	семнадцать syem**nat**sat'	
18	восемнадцать vasyem-**nat**sat'	
19	девятнадцать dyevyat**nat**sat'	
20	двадцать **dva**tsat'	

Луна-парк loona-park

колесо обозрения
kalyeso aba-zryeneeya

карусель
karoosyel'

сахарная вата
saharnaya vata

американские
горки
ameree-kanskeeye
gorkee

поезд с привидениями
poyest spreevee-dyeneeyamee

попкорн
papkorn

мат
mat

электромобили
elektra-mabeelee

набрось-кольцо
nabros'-kal'tso

американские горки
ameree-kanskeeye gorkee

54

Цирк tseerk

канатоходец
kanata-**ho**dyets

шест
shest

канат
ka**nat**

трапеция
tra**pyet**seeya

верёвочная
лестница
vye**ryo**-vachnaya
lestneetsa

батут
ba**toot**

эквилибрист
ekvee-lee**breest**

кролик
kroleek

акробаты
akra**ba**ti

дрессировщик
dryessee-**rov**shcheek

собака
sa**ba**ka

цилиндр
tsee**leen**dr

жонглёр
zhan**glyor**

кольцо
kal'**tso**

бабочка
babachka

оркестр
ar**kyes**tr

наездница
na**yez**neetsa

клоун
klo-oon

55

Word list

Here are all the Russian words in the book, in Cyrillic alphabetical order. To help you find words in the list, the Cyrillic alphabet is given below. Next to each word you can see how to pronounce it, in italics (*like this*) and then its meaning in English.

Saying Russian words

The best way to learn how to say Russian words is to listen to someone who speaks Russian and repeat what you hear. You can hear all the words in this book, read by a native Russian speaker, on the Usborne Quicklinks website. Just go to **www.usborne.com/quicklinks** and enter the keywords **1000 russian**. To help you, too, there is an easy pronunciation guide after each Russian word in the main part of book and in the list below.

Stress

In English, many words have a part that is stressed, or sounds more strongly. For example, in "window" you stress "win". It is the same in Russian, and in this book you will see that the part you stress has been shown in the pronunciation guide in bold, **like this** or *like this*. So when you read дельфин, say "dyel'**feen**" (dolphin), stressing "**feen**".

When you see the letter O, you need to notice whether it is stressed or not. If it is stressed, say "aw" as in "paw", but if it is not stressed, say "a" as in "mat". For example, when you read футбол, say "foot**bol**" (football), but when you read шоколад, say "shaka**lat**" (chocolate).

There are also six consonants that are sometimes pronounced differently, usually when they appear at the end of a word:

б   usually sounds like *b* as in *book*
    but can also sound like *p* as in *pot*
в   usually sounds like *v* as in *van*
    but can also sound like *f* as in *fan*
г   usually sounds like *g* as in *get*
    but can also sound like *k* as in *kitten*
д   usually sounds like *d* as in *day*
    but can also sound like *t* as in *teacher*
ж   usually sounds like the *s* in *pleasure*
    but can also sound like *sh* as in *show*
з   usually sounds like *z* as in *zoo*
    but can also sound like *s* as in *sit*

For example, the г in гуси (geese) is pronounced "**goos**" but in утюг (iron) it is pronounced "oot**yook**".

The letter ь is a "soft sign" – it makes the letter *before* it slightly softer. In the pronunciation guide, this is shown with an apostrophe ('), as in мать, "**mat'**" (mother). In this case, the ть sounds slightly more like *ch* as in *cheese*, rather than т on its own, which sounds like *t* as in *top*.

а б в г д е ё ж з и й к л м н о п р с т у ф х ц ч ш щ ъ ы ь э ю я

а

абрикос, 34	*abree**kos***	apricot
аварийная машина, 21	*ava**ree**naya ma**shee**na*	breakdown lorry
автобус, 12	*af**to**boos*	bus
автомойка, 21	*afta**moy**ka*	car wash
автофургон, 23	*aftafoor**gon***	caravan
айсберг, 18	***ays**byerk*	iceberg
аквариум, 29	*ak**va**reeoom*	aquarium
аккумулятор, 20	*akoomoo-**lya**tar*	battery
акробаты, 55	*akra**ba**ti*	acrobats
актёр, 40	*ak**tyor***	actor
актриса, 40	*ak**tree**sa*	actress
акула, 19	*a**koo**la*	shark
алфавит, 29	*alfa**veet***	alphabet
альпинизм, 51	*al'pee**neezm***	climbing
амбар, 24	*am**bar***	barn
американские горки, 54	*ameree-**kan**skiye **gor**kee*	rollercoaster, helter-skelter
американский футбол, 50	*ameree**kan**skiy foot**bol***	American football
ананас, 35	*ana**nas***	pineapple
антонимы, 44	*an**to**neemi*	opposites
апельсин, 31	*apel'**seen***	orange (fruit)
аэропорт, 21	*a-era**port***	airport

б

бабочка, 22	***ba**bachka*	butterfly
бабочка, 55	***ba**bachka*	bow tie
бабушка, 41	***ba**booshka*	grandmother
багажник, 21	*ba**gazh**neek*	(car) boot
бадминтон, 51	*badmeen**ton***	badminton
байдарка, 27	*bay**dar**ka*	canoe
банан, 31	*ba**nan***	banana
банка с краской, 11	***ban**ka s**kras**koy*	paint pot
банки, 11, 35	***ban**kee*	jars
барабаны, 14	*bara**ba**ni*	drums
баржа, 23	***bar**zha*	barge
барсук, 22	*bar**sook***	badger
баскетбол, 50	*baskyet**bol***	basketball
бассейн, 50	*bas**seyn***	swimming pool
батарея, 5	*bata**rye**ya*	radiator
батут, 55	*ba**toot***	safety net
бег, 50	***byek***	race
бег трусцой, 51	***byeg** troos**tsoy***	jogging
бегемот, 18	*bege**mot***	hippopotamus
бежать, 43	*bye**zhat'***	to run
бейсбол, 50	*beys**bol***	baseball
белка, 22	***byel**ka*	squirrel
белый, 52	***bye**liy*	white
белый медведь, 19	***bye**liy myed**vyet'***	polar bear
бензин, 21	*byen**zeen***	petrol
бензовоз, 21	*byenza**vos***	petrol tanker

бензоколонка, 21	byenzakalonka	petrol pump
бечёвка, 17	byechofka	string
бизон, 19	beezon	bison
бинт, 30	beent	bandage
бита, 50	beeta	bat (sports)
близко, 44	bleeska	near
блины, 36	bleeni	pancakes
блок-флейта, 14	blok-fleyta	recorder
блюдца, 7	blyootsa	saucers
бобр, 19	bobr	beaver
бобы, 35	babi	beans
божья коровка, 8	bozh'ya karofka	ladybird
больница, 30	bal'neetsa	hospital
большой, 44	bal'shoy	big
большой палец, 38	bal'shoy palyets	thumb
борьба сумо, 51	bar'ba soomo	sumo wrestling
ботинки, 39	bateenkee	shoes
бочка, 11	bochka	barrel
брат, 41	brat	brother
брать, 43	brat'	to take
брёвна, 23	bryovna	logs
брикеты соломы, 25	breekyeti salomi	straw bales
бровь, 38	brof'	eyebrow
бросать, 42	brasat'	to throw
брюки, 39	bryookee	trousers
будка, 49	bootka	kennel
булочки, 36	boolachkee	bread rolls
бумага, 29	boomaga	paper
бусы, 14	boosi	beads
бутерброд, 33	bootyerbrot	sandwich
бутылки, 35	bootilkee	bottles
буфера, 20	boofyera	buffers
бык, 24	bik	bull
быстро, 45	bistra	fast

В

в школе, 28	fshkolye	at school
вагоны, 20	vagoni	carriages
ванна, 4	vanna	bath
ванная, 4	vannaya	bathroom
варёное яйцо, 36	varyonaye yaytso	boiled egg
вата, 30	vata	cotton wool
ведро, 26	vyedro	bucket
велосипед, 13	velaseepyet	bicycle
велоспорт, 51	vyelasport	cycling
верблюд, 19	vyerblyoot	camel
верёвочная лестница, 55	vyeryo-vachnaya lestneetsa	rope ladder
верстак, 11	vyerstak	workbench
вертолёт, 20	vyertalyot	helicopter
верхний, 44	vyerhniy	top
верховая езда, 51	vyerhavaya yezda	riding
весло, 26	vyeslo	oar
весло, 27	vyeslo	paddle
весна, 48	vyesna	spring
весы, 35	vyesi	scales
ветврач, 49	vyetvrach	vet
ветер, 48	vyetyer	wind
ветки, 9	vyetkee	sticks
ветряная мельница, 22	vyetrya-naya myel'neetsa	windmill
ветчина, 37	vyetcheena	ham
вечер, 46	vyecher	evening
вечеринка, 32	vyechereenka	party
вешалка, 5	vyeshalka	pegs
вёсельная лодка, 27	vyosel'naya lotka	rowing boat
взлётная полоса, 21	vslyotnaya palasa	runway
вилки, 6	veelkee	forks
вилы, 9	veeli	(garden) fork
виндсёрфинг, 50	veendsyorfeenk	windsurfing

виноград, 31	veenagrat	grapes
винты, 11	veenti	bolts
вишня, 33	veeshnya	cherry
внизу, 45	vneezoo	downstairs
внутри, 45	vnootree	in
вода, 4	vada	water
водитель автобуса, 41	vadeetyel' avtoboosa	bus driver
водитель грузовика, 41	vadeetyel' groozaveeka	lorry driver
водный лыжник, 26	vodniy lizhneek	water-skier
водолаз, 41	vadalas	diver
водопад, 23	vadapat	waterfall
водоросли, 27	vodaraslee	seaweed
воздушный змей, 16	vazdooshniy zmyey	kite
воздушный шар, 22	vazdooshniy shar	hot-air balloon
воздушный шарик, 32	vazdooshniy shareek	balloon
вокзал, 20	vakzal	railway station
волк, 18	volk	wolf
волнистый попугай, 49	valneestiy papoo-gay	budgerigar
волны, 27	volni	waves
волосы, 38	volasi	hair
восемнадцать, 53	vasyem-natsat'	eighteen
восемь, 53	vosyem'	eight
восковые мелки, 29	vaskaviye myelkee	crayons
воскресенье, 46	vaskre-syen'ye	Sunday
врач, 30, 31	vrach	doctor
времена года, 48	vremyena goda	seasons
вторник, 46	ftorneek	Tuesday
выключатель, 6	viklyoo-chatyel'	switch
высоко, 45	visako	high
вязать, 42	vyazat'	to knit

Г

гаечный ключ, 21	gayechniy klyooch	spanner
газета, 5	gazyeta	newspaper
газонокосилка, 9	gazona-kaseelka	lawnmower
гайки, 11	gaykee	nuts
галстук, 39	galstook	tie
галька, 27	gal'ka	pebbles
гамбургер, 37	gamboorgyer	hamburger
гараж, 20	garash	garage
гвозди, 11	gvozdee	nails
гимнастика, 50	geemnasteeka	gymnastics
гипс, 30	geeps	plaster cast
гирлянда, 32	geerlyanda	paper chain
гитара, 14	geetara	guitar
гладильная доска, 6	gladeel'naya daska	ironing board
глаз, 38	glas	eye
глина, 28	gleena	modelling clay
глобус, 29	globoos	globe
гнездо, 9	gnyezdo	bird's nest
голова, 38	galava	head
головастики, 16	galavasteekee	tadpoles
голубь, 8	goloop'	pigeon
гоночная машина, 15	gonachnaya masheena	racing car
гора, 22	gara	mountain
горилла, 18	gareella	gorilla
горка для катания, 16	gorka dlya kataneeya	ski slope
горох, 34	garoh	peas
горячий, 44	garyachee	hot
гости, 47	gostee	guests
гостиная, 4	gasteenaya	living room
гостиница, 12	gasteeneetsa	hotel
готовить еду, 43	gatoveet' yedoo	to cook
грабли, 9	grablee	rake

гребля, 50	*gryeblya*	rowing
грейпфрут, 34	*greypfroot*	grapefruit
гриб, 34	*greep*	mushroom
грим, 15	*greem*	face paints
грудь, 38	*groot'*	chest
грузовик, 13	*groozaveek*	lorry
груша, 31	*groosha*	pear
грязный, 44	*gryazniy*	dirty
губка, 4	*goopka*	sponge
губная гармошка, 14	*goobnaya garmoshka*	mouth organ
губы, 38	*goobi*	lips
гусеница, 9	*goosyeneetsa*	caterpillar
гуси, 24	*goosee*	geese

Д

DVD-диск	*dee-vee-dee deesk*	DVD
далеко, 44	*dalyeko*	far
два, 53	*dva*	two
двадцать, 53	*dvatsat'*	twenty
двенадцать, 53	*dvyenatsat'*	twelve
дверная ручка, 29	*dvyernaya roochka*	door handle
дверь, 6	*dver'*	door
двигатель, 20	*dveegatyel'*	(car) engine
двоюродный брат, 41	*dvayooradniy brat*	cousin
девочка, 29	*dyevachka*	girl
девятнадцать, 53	*dyevyatnatsat'*	nineteen
девять, 53	*dyevyat'*	nine
Дед Мороз, 47	*dyet maros*	Father Christmas
дедушка, 41	*dyedooshka*	grandfather
делать, 42	*dyelat'*	to make
дельтапланеризм, 51	*dyel'ta-planyereezm*	hang-gliding
дельфин, 18	*dyel'feen*	dolphin
день рождения, 47	*dyen' razhdyeneeya*	birthday
деньги, 35	*dyen'gee*	money
деревня, 23	*deryevnya*	village
дерево, 9	*dyereva*	tree
деревья, 17	*dyerev'ya*	trees
десерт, 37	*desyert*	pudding
десять, 53	*dyesyat'*	ten
дети, 17	*dyetee*	children
джем, 36	*djem*	jam
джемпер, 39	*djempyer*	jumper
джинсы, 39	*djeensi*	jeans
дзюдо, 51	*dzyoodo*	judo
диспетчерская вышка, 21	*deespyetcherskaya vishka*	control tower
длинный, 45	*dleenniy*	long
дни, 46	*dnee*	days
дождь, 48	*dosht'*	rain
дом, 13	*dom*	house, block of flats
дом на ферме, 25	*dom na fyermye*	farmhouse
дома, 4	*doma*	at home
домашнее животное, 41	*damashnyeye zhivotnoye*	pet
домашние животные, 49	*damashneeye zhivotniye*	pets
дорога, 22	*daroga*	road
дорожный указатель, 22	*darozhniy ookazatyel'*	signpost
доска, 10	*daska*	plank
доска, 28	*daska*	board
дочь, 41	*doch'*	daughter
драться, 43	*drat'sa*	to fight
дрель, 10	*dryel'*	(hand) drill
дрессировщик, 55	*dryessee-rovshcheek*	ringmaster
дрова, 11	*drava*	wood
думать, 42	*doomat'*	to think
дуть, 43	*doot'*	to blow
душ, 4	*doosh*	shower
дым, 9	*dim*	smoke
дыня, 34	*dinya*	melon
дядя, 41	*dyadya*	uncle

е

еда, 36	*yeda*	food
есть, 42	*yest'*	to eat

ё

ёж, 22	*yosh*	hedgehog
ёлка, 47	*yolka*	Christmas tree

Ж

жаба, 23	*zhaba*	toad
жалюзи, 29	*zhalyoozee*	(window) blind
ждать, 43	*zhdat'*	to wait
железная дорога, 14, 20	*zhelyeznaya daroga*	train set, railway track
жена, 41	*zhena*	wife
жених, 47	*zheneeh*	bridegroom
женщина, 13	*zhenshcheena*	woman
женщина-полицейский, 40	*zhenshcheena-palitsyeyskiy*	policewoman
жёлтый, 52	*zholtiy*	yellow
живая изгородь, 9	*zhivaya eezgarad'*	hedge
живой, 45	*zhivoy*	alive
живот, 38	*zhivot*	tummy
животные, 18	*zhivotniye*	animals
жираф, 18	*zhiraf*	giraffe
жонглёр, 55	*zhanglyor*	juggler

З

забор, 17	*zabor*	railings
забор, 25	*zabor*	fence
завтрак, 36	*zaftrak*	breakfast
закрытый, 44	*zakritiy*	closed
залезать, 43	*zalyezat'*	to climb
замок, 14	*zamak*	castle
замок из песка, 26	*zamak eez pyeska*	sandcastle
занавеска, 30	*zana-vyeska*	curtain
занятия, 42	*zanyateeya*	doing things
звезда, 46, 52	*zvyezda*	star
зебра, 19	*zyebra*	zebra
зелёный, 52	*zyelyoniy*	green
земля, 17	*zyemlya*	earth
земля, 24	*zyemlya*	mud
зеркало, 5	*zyerkala*	mirror
зима, 48	*zeema*	winter
змея, 19	*zmeya*	snake
значок, 29	*znachok*	badge
золотые рыбки, 49	*zalatiye ripkee*	goldfish
зонтик, 26, 48	*zonteek*	umbrella
зубная паста, 4	*zoobnaya pasta*	toothpaste
зубная щётка, 4	*zoobnaya shchotka*	toothbrush
зубной врач, 41	*zoobnoy vrach*	dentist
зубы, 38	*zoobi*	teeth

И

игральные карты, 15	*eegral'niye karti*	(playing) cards
игральные кости, 14	*eegral'niye kostee*	dice
играть, 43	*eegrat'*	to play
игрушки, 31, 32	*eegrooshkee*	toys
идти, 43	*eedtee*	to walk
индюки, 25	*eendyookee*	turkeys

58

огурт, 35	yogoort	yoghurt

К

акао, 36	kakao	hot chocolate
алендарь, 10, 46	kalyendar'	calendar
алитка, 16	kaleetka	gate
амни, 22	kamnee	stones
амни, 23	kamnee	rocks
анал, 23	kanal	canal
анарейка, 49	kanaryeyka	canary
анат, 27	kanat	rope
анат, 55	kanat	tightrope
анатоходец, 55	kanata-hodyets	tightrope walker
апот , 21	kapot	(car) bonnet
апуста, 34	kapoosta	cabbage
арандаш, 28	karandash	pencil
аратэ, 50	karate	karate
арманы, 39	karmani	pockets
арта, 29	karta	map
артинка-конструктор, 30	karteenka-kanstrooktar	jigsaw
артины, 5	karteeni	pictures
артофель, 35, 37	kartofel'	potatoes
артофельное пюре, 37	kartofel'naye pyoore	mashed potatoes
арусель, 54	karoosyel'	roundabout
асса, 35	kassa	checkout
асса-автомат, 20	kassa-aftamat	ticket machine
астрюли, 6	kastryoolee	saucepans
атер, 26	katyer	motor-boat
аток, 13, 15	katok	roller
афе, 12	ka-fe	cafe
афель, 7	kafyel'	tiles
ачели, 16	kachyelee	swings
ачели, 17	kachyelee	seesaw
вадрат, 52	kvadrat	square
енгуру, 18	kengooroo	kangaroo
епка, 39	kyepka	cap
инотеатр, 13	keenateatr	cinema
ирпичи, 8	keerpeechee	bricks
источка, 29	keestachka	paintbrush
исть руки, 38	keest' rookee	hand
ит, 19	keet	whale
ладовка, 7	kladofka	cupboard
лей, 28	kley	glue
летка, 49	klyetka	cage
лоун, 55	klo-oon	clown
лубника, 33	kloobneeka	strawberry
лумба, 17	kloomba	flower bed
люв, 49	klyoof	beak
люч, 6	klyooch	key
ниги, 28	kneegee	books
нопки, 11	knopkee	tacks
овёр, 4	kavyor	carpet
оврик, 5	kovreek	rug
оза, 19	kaza	goat
олготки, 39	kalgotkee	tights
олено, 38	kalyena	knee
олесо, 20	kalyeso	wheel
олесо обозрения, 54	kalyeso aba-zryeneeya	big wheel
олли, 24	kollee	sheepdog
ольцо, 14	kal'tso	ring
ольцо, 55	kal'tso	hoop
оляска, 9	kalyaska	pram
омиксы, 31	komeeksi	comic
омод, 5	kamot	chest of drawers
омпакт-диск, 4	kampakt deesk	CD
омпьютер, 31	kamp'yooter	computer
консервы, 35	kansyervi	tins
контролёр, 20	kantralyor	ticket inspector
конус, 52	konoos	cone
конфета, 32	kanfyeta	sweet
коньки, 51	kan'kee	ice skates
конюшня, 25	kanyooshnya	stable
копать, 42	kapat'	to dig
копилка, 15	kapeelka	money box
корабль, 27	karabl'	ship
корзина, 31, 35, 49	karzeena	basket
коричневый, 52	kareechnyeviy	brown
корм, 49	korm	petfood
коробка, 29	karopka	box
корова, 25	karova	cow
коровник, 25	karovneek	cowshed
короткий, 45	karotkee	short
космонавт, 40	kasmanaft	astronaut
космонавты, 15	kasmanafti	spacemen
космос, 46	kosmas	space
костёр, 9	kastyor	bonfire
костыли, 30	kastilee	crutches
кость, 9	kost'	bone
котёнок, 49	katyonak	kitten
кофе, 36	kofye	coffee
кофта, 39	kofta	cardigan
кошелёк, 35	kashelyok	purse
кошка, 49	koshka	cat
краб, 26	krap	crab
кран, 4	kran	tap
краски, 15, 28	kraskee	paints
красный, 52	krasniy	red
кресло-каталка, 30	kryesla-katalka	wheelchair
крикет, 50	kreekyet	cricket
кровать, 4	kravat'	bed
крокодил, 18	krakadeel	crocodile
кролик, 49, 55	kroleek	rabbit
кроссовки, 39	krassofkee	trainers
крот, 23	krot	mole
круг, 52	krook	circle
крыло, 18	krilo	wing
крыша, 12	krisha	roof
куб, 52	koop	cube
кубики, 14	koobeekee	building blocks
куклы, 14	kookli	dolls
кукольный дом, 14	kookal'niy dom	doll's house
купальник, 27	koopal'neek	swimsuit
куртка, 39	koortka	jacket
куры, 25	koori	hens
курятник, 24	kooryatneek	henhouse
куст, 16	koost	bush
кухня, 6	koohnya	kitchen
кухонное полотенце, 7	koohannaye palatyentse	tea towel

Л

лампа, 5	lampa	lamp
лампочка, 33	lampachka	light bulb
лапы, 18	lapi	paws
ласты, 27	lasti	flippers
лебеди, 17	lyebedee	swans
лев, 18	lyef	lion
левый, 44	lyeviy	left
легко, 45	lyehko	easy
лейка, 8	leyka	watering can
лекарство, 30	lyekarstva	medicine
лента, 32	lyenta	ribbon
леопард, 19	lyeapart	leopard
лес, 22	lyes	forest
лестница, 5	lyesneetsa	stairs
лестница, 10	lyesneetsa	ladder
лестница, 13	lyesneetsa	steps

лето, 48	*lyeta*	summer
летучая мышь, 18	*lyetoochaya mish'*	bat (animal)
лимон, 34	*leemon*	lemon
линейка, 28	*leenyeyka*	ruler
лиса, 22	*leesa*	fox
листья, 9	*leest'ya*	leaves
лисята, 23	*leesyata*	fox cubs
лифт, 30	*leeft*	lift
лицо, 38	*leetso*	face
ловить, 42	*laveet'*	to catch
ложки, 7	*loshkee*	spoons
локомотив, 20	*lakamateef*	(train) engine
локоть, 38	*lokat'*	elbow
ломать, 42	*lamat'*	to break
лопата, 8, 26	*lapata*	spade
лошадь, 25, 51	*loshat'*	horse
лошадь-качалка, 15	*loshat'-kachalka*	rocking horse
лужа, 17	*loozha*	puddle
лук, 15	*look*	bow
лук, 34	*look*	onion
лук-порей, 34	*look-parey*	leek
луна, 46	*loona*	moon
луна-парк, 54	*loona-park*	fairground
лыжи, 51	*lizhee*	skis
лыжная палка, 51	*lizhnaya palka*	ski pole
львята, 18	*l'vyata*	lion cubs
люди, 40	*lyoodee*	people
лягушка, 16	*lyagooshka*	frog

M

магазин, 12, 34	*magazeen*	shop
магазин игрушек, 14	*magazeen eegrooshek*	toyshop
майка, 39	*mayka*	vest
маленький, 44	*malyen'kiy*	small
малина, 33	*maleena*	raspberry
мало, 44	*mala*	few
малыш, 17	*malish*	baby
мальчик, 28	*mal'cheek*	boy
маляр, 41	*malyar*	painter
мандарин, 33	*mandareen*	clementine
марионетки, 15	*mareea-nyetkee*	puppets
маскарадные костюмы, 33	*maska-radniye kastyoomi*	fancy dress
маски, 15	*maskee*	masks
масло, 21	*masla*	oil
масло, 33	*masla*	butter
мастерская, 10	*mastyerskaya*	workshop
мат, 54	*mat*	mat
мать, 41	*mat'*	mother
машина, 13	*masheena*	car
машинист, 20	*masheeneest*	train driver
маяк, 26	*mayak*	lighthouse
медбрат, 30	*myedbrat*	(male) nurse
медведь, 18	*myedvyet'*	bear
медленно, 45	*myedlyenna*	slow
мел, 28	*myel*	chalk
механики, 40	*myehaneekee*	mechanics
мёд, 36	*myot*	honey
мёртвый, 45	*myortviy*	dead
миски, 7	*meeskee*	bowls
мишень, 51	*meeshyen'*	target
много, 44	*mnoga*	many
мойка, 6	*moyka*	sink
мокрый, 44	*mokriy*	wet
молния, 39	*molneeya*	zip
молния, 48	*molneeya*	lightning
молоко, 36, 49	*malako*	milk
молоток, 11	*malatok*	hammer
мольберт, 29	*mal'byert*	easel

море, 26	*morye*	sea
морковь, 34	*markof'*	carrot
мороженое, 16	*marozhenaye*	ice cream
мороз, 48	*maros*	frost
морская звезда, 26	*marskaya zvyezda*	starfish
морская свинка, 49	*marskaya sveenka*	guinea pig
моряк, 26	*maryak*	sailor
мост, 23	*most*	bridge
мотоцикл, 13	*matatseekl*	motorcycle
мотыга, 8	*matiga*	hoe
мотылёк, 23	*matilyok*	moth
моя, 39	*maya*	my
муж, 41	*moosh*	husband
мужчина, 12	*mooshcheena*	man
мука, 35	*mooka*	flour
мусор, 6	*moosar*	rubbish
мусорное ведро, 29	*moosarnaye vyedro*	wastepaper bin
мусорный бак, 8	*moosarniy bak*	dustbin
муха, 11	*mooha*	fly
мыло, 4	*mila*	soap
мыть, 42	*mit'*	to wash
мышь, 49	*mish'*	mouse
мягкий, 45	*myahkee*	soft
мясник, 40	*myasneek*	butcher
мясо, 35	*myasa*	meat
мяч, 17, 50	*myach*	ball

Н

набрось-кольцо, 54	*nabros'-kal'tso*	hoop-la
наверху, 45	*navyerhoo*	upstairs
над, 44	*nat*	over
наездница, 55	*nayezneetsa*	bareback rider
наждачная бумага, 10	*nazhdachnaya boomaga*	sandpaper
наживка, 50	*nazhifka*	bait
напильник, 11	*napeel'neek*	file
настольная лампа, 29	*nastol'naya lampa*	desk lamp
настольный теннис, 51	*nastol'niy tennees*	table tennis
небо, 48	*nyeba*	sky
невеста, 47	*nyevyesta*	bride
нести, 42	*nyestee*	to carry
нижний, 44	*neezhnee*	bottom (not top)
низко, 45	*neezka*	low
новый, 45	*noviy*	new
нога, 38	*naga*	leg
ножи, 7	*nazhee*	knives
ножницы, 28	*nozhneetsi*	scissors
нос, 38	*nos*	nose
носки, 39	*naskee*	socks
носовой платок, 39	*nasavoy platok*	handkerchief
носорог, 19	*nasarok*	rhinoceros
ночная рубашка, 31	*nachnaya roobashka*	nightdress
ночь, 46	*noch'*	night

О

обед, 36	*abyet*	lunch
обезьяна, 18	*abyez'yana*	monkey
облака, 48	*oblaka*	clouds
овал, 52	*aval*	oval
овощи, 9, 34	*ovashchee*	vegetables
овцы, 25	*oftsi*	sheep
огурец, 34	*agooryets*	cucumber
одежда, 39	*adyezhda*	clothes
один, 53	*adeen*	one
одиннадцать, 53	*adeennatsat'*	eleven
ожерелье, 14	*azheryel'ye*	necklace
озеро, 16	*ozyera*	lake
окно, 32	*akno*	window

61

пряжка, 39	*pryashka*	buckle
прямоугольник, 52	*pryama-oogol'neek*	rectangle
прятаться, 43	*pryatat'sa*	to hide
птицы, 17	*pteetsi*	birds
пугало, 25	*poogala*	scarecrow
пуговицы, 39	*poogaveetsi*	buttons
пурпурный, 52	*poorpoorniy*	purple
пустой, 45	*poostoy*	empty
путешествие, 20	*pootye-shestveeye*	travel
пуховое одеяло, 5	*poohovaye adyeyala*	duvet
пчела, 9	*pchyela*	bee
пылесос, 6	*pilyesos*	vacuum cleaner
пятнадцать, 53	*pyatnatsat'*	fifteen
пятница, 46	*pyatneetsa*	Friday
пять, 53	*pyat'*	five

р

радио, 4	*radeeo*	radio
радуга, 48	*radooga*	rainbow
разговаривать, 42	*razga-vareevat'*	to talk
раздевалка, 51	*razdye-valka*	changing room
ракета, 15	*rakyeta*	rocket
ракета, 46	*rakyeta*	spaceship
ракетка, 50	*rakyetka*	racket
раковина, 4	*rakaveena*	basin
ракушка, 26	*rakooshka*	shell
растение, 29	*rastyeneeye*	plant
расчёска, 5	*raschoska*	comb
регби, 50	*regbee*	rugby
резать, 42	*ryezat'*	to cut
резинка, 28	*ryezeenka*	rubber
река, 22	*ryeka*	river
ремень, 39	*ryemen'*	belt
рис, 37	*rees*	rice
рисовать, 42	*reesavat'*	to paint
рисунок, 28	*reesoonak*	drawing
робот, 14	*robat*	robot
Рождество, 47	*razhdestvo*	Christmas day
рожки, 19	*rozhkee*	horns
розовый, 52	*rozoviy*	pink
ролики, 16	*roleekee*	roller blades
ромб, 52	*romp*	diamond
роса, 48	*rasa*	dew
рот, 38	*rot*	mouth
рояль, 15	*rayal'*	piano
рубанок, 11	*roobanak*	shaving plane
рубашка, 39	*roobashka*	shirt
рубить, 42	*roobeet'*	to chop
рука, 38	*rooka*	arm
рулетка, 11	*roolyetka*	tape measure
ручей, 22	*roochey*	stream
ручка, 28	*roochka*	pen
рыба, 27	*riba*	fish
рыбак, 23	*ribak*	fisherman
рыбалка, 50	*ribalka*	fishing
рыбачья лодка, 27	*ribach'ya lotka*	fishing boat
рынок, 13	*rinak*	market
рюкзак, 20	*ryookzak*	backpack

с

сад, 8	*sat*	garden
сад, 25	*sat*	orchard
салат, 34	*salat*	lettuce
салат, 37	*salat*	salad
салфетки, 31	*salfyetkee*	tissues
салями, 33	*salyamee*	salami
самолёт, 21	*samalyot*	plane
сандали, 39	*sandalee*	sandals
сани, 47	*sanee*	sleigh
сапоги, 39	*sapagee*	boots
сарай, 8	*saray*	shed
сахар, 36	*sahar*	sugar
сахарная вата, 54	*saharnaya vata*	candy floss
свадьба, 47	*svad'ba*	wedding day
светло, 45	*svyetlo*	light
светофор, 13	*svyetafor*	traffic lights
свеча, 32, 47	*svyecha*	candle
свинарник, 24	*sveenarneek*	pigsty
свиньи, 25	*sveen'ee*	pigs
свисток, 14	*sveestok*	whistle
свитер, 39	*sveeter*	sweatshirt
северный олень, 47	*syeverniy alen'*	reindeer
седло, 25	*syedlo*	saddle
сельдерей, 34	*syel'derey*	celery
сельская местность, 22	*syel'skaya myestnast'*	country
семафор, 20	*semafor*	signals
семена, 8	*syemena*	seeds
семнадцать, 53	*syemnatsat'*	seventeen
семь, 53	*syem'*	seven
семья, 41	*syem'ya*	family
сено, 25	*syena*	hay
серый, 52	*syeriy*	grey
сестра, 41	*syestra*	sister
сеть, 27	*syet'*	net
сзади, 45	*szadee*	behind
сидеть, 43	*seedyet'*	to sit
синий, 52	*seenee*	blue
скакалка, 17	*skakalka*	skipping rope
скамейка, 16	*skamyeyka*	bench
скатерть, 33	*skatyert'*	tablecloth
скейтборд, 17	*skeytbort*	skateboard
сковорода, 7	*skavarada*	frying pan
скорая помощь, 12	*skoraya pomashch'*	ambulance
слива, 35	*sleeva*	plum
сливки, 36	*sleefkee*	cream
слон, 19	*slon*	elephant
слушать, 42	*slooshat'*	to listen
смеяться, 42	*smeyat'sa*	to laugh
смотреть, 43	*smatryet'*	to watch
снаружи, 45	*snaroozhee*	out
снег, 48	*snyek*	snow
сноубординг, 50	*sno-oobordeenk*	snowboarding
собака, 16, 49, 55	*sabaka*	dog
собирать, 43	*sabeerat'*	to pick
сова, 23	*sava*	owl
совок, 7	*savok*	dustpan
совок, 9	*savok*	trowel
солдатики, 15	*saldateekee*	soldiers
солнце, 46, 48	*sontse*	sun
соломинка, 32	*salomeenka*	straw
соль, 36	*sol'*	salt
сосиска, 33	*saseeska*	sausage
соус, 37	*so-oos*	sauce
софа, 4	*safa*	sofa
спагетти, 37	*spagettee*	spaghetti
спальня, 5	*spal'nya*	bedroom
спать, 43	*spat'*	to sleep
спереди, 45	*speryedee*	in front
спина, 38	*speena*	back (of body)
спички, 7	*speechkee*	matches
спорт, 50	*sport*	sport
среда, 46	*sryeda*	Wednesday
стаканы, 6	*stakani*	glasses (for drinking)
старый, 45	*stariy*	old
стена, 29	*styena*	wall
стиральная машина, 7	*steeral'naya masheena*	washing mashine
стиральный порошок, 6	*steeral'niy parashok*	washing powder
стог, 24	*stok*	haystack

тол, 5	**stol**	table
траус, 18	**stra**oos	ostrich
трелы, 14	**stry**eli	arrows
трельба из лука, 51	stryel'**ba** eez **loo**ka	archery
тружки, 10	**stroosh**kee	shavings
тул, 5	**stool**	chair
тупня, 38	**stoop**nya	foot
тюарды, 21	styoo**ar**dy	cabin crew
уббота, 46	soob**bo**ta	Saturday
удья, 40	sood'**ya**	judge
умочка, 35	**soo**machka	handbag
уп, 37	**soop**	soup
ухой, 44	soo**hoy**	dry
ын, 41	**sin**	son
ыр, 33, 34	**seer**	cheese

аблетки, 30	ta**blyet**kee	pills
абурет, 6	taboo**ryet**	stool
акси, 13	tak**see**	taxi
анкер, 27	**tan**kyer	oil tanker (ship)
анцевать, 42	tantse**vat'**	to dance
анцоры, 40	tan**tso**ri	dancers
анцы, 50	**tan**tsi	dance
арелки, 7	ta**ryel**kee	plates
ачка, 8	**tach**ka	wheelbarrow
вёрдый, 45	**tvyor**diy	hard
елевизор, 5	tele**vee**zar	television
ележка, 24	tye**lyesh**ka	cart
ележка, 35	tye**lyesh**ka	trolley
елескоп, 46	tye**les**kop	telescope
елефон, 5	tele**fon**	telephone
елёнок, 25	tye**lyo**nak	calf
емно, 45	**tyem**no	dark
еннис, 50	**ten**nees	tennis
еплица, 9	tye**pleet**sa	greenhouse
ермометр, 30	tyer**mo**metr	thermometer
етрадь, 29	tye**trat'**	notebook
ётя, 41	**tyo**tya	aunt
игр, 19	**tee**gr	tiger
иски, 10	tee**skee**	vice
оварный поезд, 20	ta**var**niy **po**yest	goods train
олкать, 43	tal**kat'**	to push
олстый, 44	**tol**stiy	fat
онкий, 44	**ton**kee	thin
опор, 11	ta**por**	axe
орт, 32	**tort**	cake
осты, 36	**tos**ti	toast
рава, 9	tra**va**	grass
рактор, 24	**trak**tar	tractor
рапеция, 55	tra**pyet**seeya	trapeze
реугольник, 52	trye-oo**gol'**neek	triangle
рёхколесный велосипед, 17	tryohkal-**yos**niy vyela-see**pyet**	tricycle
ри, 53	**tree**	three
ринадцать, 53	tree**nat**sat'	thirteen
ропинка, 9, 16	tra**peen**ka	path
ротуар, 12	tra**too**ar	pavement
руба, 12	troo**ba**	chimney
руба, 14	troo**ba**	trumpet
рубы, 12	**troo**bi	pipes
рудно, 45	**trood**na	difficult
русы, 39	troo**see**	pants
ряпка для пыли, 7	**tryap**ka dlya **pi**lee	duster
уалетная бумага, 4	tooa**lyet**-naya boo**ma**ga	toilet paper
уман, 48	too**man**	fog, mist
уннель, 23	too**nel'**	tunnel
ыква, 35	**tik**va	pumpkin
юлень, 19	tyoo**len'**	seal
януть, 43	tya**noot'**	to pull

У

у моря, 26	oo **mor**ya	at the seaside
удочка, 50	**oo**dachka	fishing rod
ужин, 37	**oo**zheen	dinner, supper
улей, 8	**oo**ley	beehive
улитка, 8	oo**leet**ka	snail
улица, 12	**oo**leetsa	street
уличный фонарь, 13	**oo**leechniy fa**nar'**	lamp post
улыбаться, 42	ooli**bat'**sa	to smile
унитаз, 4	oonee**tas**	toilet
утёс, 27	oo**tyos**	cliff
утки, 17	**oot**kee	ducklings
утро, 46	**oo**tra	morning
утюг, 7	oo**tyook**	iron
утята, 17	oo**tya**ta	ducks
учительница, 29	oo**chee**tel'neetsa	teacher
уши, 38	**oo**shee	ears

Ф

фабрика, 13	**fa**breeka	factory
фартук, 6	**far**took	apron
фары, 20	**fa**ri	headlights
фейерверк, 32	feyer**vyerk**	fireworks
ферма, 24	**fyer**ma	farm
фермер, 25	**fyer**myer	farmer
фигурное катание, 51	fee**goor**naye ka**ta**neeye	ice-skating
фигуры, 52	fee**goo**ri	shapes
физкультура, 50	feeskool'-**too**ra	exercise
флаг, 26	**flak**	flag
фломастеры, 28	fla**mas**teri	felt-tips
фотоаппарат, 14, 47	fota-appa**rat**	camera
фотограф, 47	fa**to**graf	photographer
фотографии, 28	fata**gra**fee	photographs
фруктовый сок, 33	frook**to**viy **sok**	fruit juice
фрукты, 5, 34	**frook**ti	fruit
фургон, 13	foor**gon**	van
футбол, 51	foot**bol**	football
футболка, 39	foot**bol**ka	T-shirt

Х

халат, 30	ha**lat**	dressing gown
хвост, 18	**hvost**	tail
хлеб, 33	**hlyep**	bread
хлопья, 36	**hlop'**ya	cereal
хобот, 19	**ho**bat	trunk
холл, 5	**holl**	hall
холм, 23	**holm**	hill
холодильник, 6	hala**deel'**neek	fridge
холодный, 44	ha**lod**niy	cold
хомяк, 49	ha**myak**	hamster
хороший, 44	ha**ro**shee	good
художник, 40	hoo**dozh**neek	artist

Ц

цвета, 52	tsvye**ta**	colours
цветная капуста, 34	tsvyet**na**ya ka**poos**ta	cauliflower
цветы, 8	tsvye**ti**	flowers
цилиндр, 55	tsee**leen**dr	top hat
цирк, 55	**tseerk**	circus
цистерна, 24	tsees**ter**na	tanker (lorry)
цыплёнок, 37	tsi**plyo**nak	chicken
цыплята, 24	tsi**plya**ta	chicks

Ч

чай, 36	**chay**	tea
чайка, 26	**chay**ka	seagull

чайник, 7	**chay**neek	kettle
чайник, 36	**chay**neek	teapot
чайные ложки, 6	**chay**niye **lozh**kee	teaspoons
часы, 6	cha**si**	clock
часы, 30	cha**si**	watch
чашки, 7	**chash**kee	cups
чемодан, 20	chema**dan**	suitcase
червяк, 8	cher**vyak**	worm
чердак, 24	cher**dak**	loft
черепаха, 19	chere**pa**ha	tortoise
четверг, 46	chet**vyerk**	Thursday
четыре, 53	che**tir**ye	four
четырнадцать, 53	che**tir**-natsat'	fourteen
чёрный, 52	**chor**niy	black
чипсы, 33	**cheep**si	crisps
чипсы, 37	**cheep**si	chips
числа, 53	**chees**la	numbers
чистый, 44	**chees**tiy	clean
читать, 43	chee**tat'**	to read

Ш

шарики, 15	**sha**reekee	marbles
шарф, 39	**sharf**	scarf
швабра, 7	**shva**bra	mop
шезлонг, 27	shez**lonk**	deck chair
шест, 55	**shest**	pole
шестнадцать, 53	shest**nat**sat'	sixteen
шесть, 53	**shest'**	six
шея, 38	**she**ya	neck
шина, 21	**shee**na	tyre
шить, 43	**sheet'**	to sew
шкаф, 5	**shkaf**	wardrobe
шкафчик, 51	**shkaf**cheek	locker
школа, 12	**shko**la	school
шланг, 9	**shlank**	hosepipe
шлем, 51	**shlyem**	helmet
шлёпанцы, 31	**shlyo**pantsi	slippers
шлюз, 22	**shlyoos**	lock
шляпа, 27	**shlya**pa	sunhat

шляпа, 39	**shlya**pa	hat
шнурок, 39	shnoo**rok**	shoelace
шоколад, 32	shaka**lad**	chocolate
шорты, 39	**shor**ti	shorts
шпинат, 35	shpee**nat**	spinach
шприц, 30	**shpreets**	syringe
шурупы, 10	shoo**roo**pi	screws

Щ

щека, 38	shche**ka**	cheek
щенок, 49	shche**nok**	puppy
щётка, 5, 7	**shchot**ka	brush
щётка, 7	**shchot**ka	broom

Э

эквилибрист, 55	ekvee-lee**breest**	trick cyclist
экскаватор, 12	ekska**va**tar	digger
электромобили, 54	elektra-ma**bee**lee	dodgems

Ю

юбка, 39	**yoop**ka	skirt

Я

я, 38	**ya**	me, I
яблоко, 30	**ya**blaka	apple
ягнята, 24	yag**nya**ta	lambs
ягодицы, 38	yaga**deet**si	bottom (of body)
язык, 38	ya**zik**	tongue
яичница, 36	ya**eesh**neetsa	fried egg
яйца, 35	**yay**tsa	eggs
яма, 12	**ya**ma	hole
яхта, 15, 17	**yah**ta	yacht
ящерица, 22	**yash**chereetsa	lizard
ящик, 7	**yash**cheek	drawer
ящик для инструментов, 10	**yash**cheek dlya eenstroo-**myen**taf	tool box